W9-CSC-760

CREATE YOUR OWN CANDLES

30 EASY-TO-MAKE DESIGNS

LAURA CHECK

ILLUSTRATIONS BY NORMA JEAN MARTIN-JOURDENAIS

Quick Starts for Kids!®

WILLIAMSON BOOKS   NASHVILLE, TENNESSEE

Library of Congress Cataloging-in-Publication Data

Check, Laura, 1958-
    Create your own candles : 30 easy-to-make designs / Laura Check ; illustrations by
    Norma Jean Martin-Jourdenais
        p. cm. — (Quick starts for kids!)
    Includes index.
    ISBN: 0-8249-8663-6 (pbk.)
        1. Candlemaking—Juvenile literature. I. Title. II. Series.

TT896.5.C455 2004
745.593'32—dc22   2004040870

Quick Starts for Kids!® series editor: **Susan Williamson**
Project editor: **Vicky Congdon**
Interior design: **Linda Williamson, Dawson Design**
Illustrations: **Norma Jean Martin-Jourdenais**
Cover design: **Sarah Rakitin**
Cover photography: **Karen Pike Photography**

Published by Williamson Books
An imprint of Ideals Publications
A division of Guideposts
535 Metroplex Drive, Suite 250
Nashville, Tennessee 37211
800-586-2572

Manufactured in the United States of America

10 9 8 7 6 5 4 3 2 1

DEDICATION

THIS BOOK IS DEDICATED
TO MY HUSBAND, TOM:
I LOVE MY WORKSHOP!

ACKNOWLEDGMENT

I'd like to thank Ginger from Island Soap & Candle Works in Kilauea, Hawaii, for sharing some of her candle ideas and techniques with me — Ginger, your shop is fantastic! I'd also like to thank Kula Elementary School for donating the beeswax sheets and to everyone at Williamson Publishing for contributing her favorite candle ideas.

CONTENTS

Let's Make Candles!

I used to think making candles would be too complicated and would require all kinds of special equipment. But after experimenting over the years, I've discovered candle making is quite simple and other than wax, wicks, and a few other supplies, there is very little I have to buy. It has become one of my favorite hobbies!

Candle making has come a long way from the smoky, smelly days of boiling down animal fats to make tallow (wax). Today wax and candle-making supplies are readily available. But the techniques of making candles have stayed basically the same: Candles are either dipped, poured into a mold, or rolled. It's easy to create an assortment of wonderful candles in all shapes and sizes to be given as gifts; used for birthdays, celebrations, and ceremonies; or just enjoyed for the beauty and warm glow they add to any room.

My first concern, however, in sharing my candle-crafting designs and techniques with you is your safety. Please read over the Ten Hot Safety Tips (page 6) to prevent any accidents and remember to always have adult supervision as candle crafting does involve hot wax or gel. If you invent candle designs of your own (and I hope you will!), or change any of mine to suit your personal tastes, never use any flammable materials for decorations. If you're not sure, check with an adult.

After that, just let your imagination loose and enjoy the amazing combinations of colors, shapes, sizes, and designs that is the world of handcrafted candles!

Laura Check

Before You Start: Candle-Making Supplies

andle making doesn't need to be expensive. I've collected most of my supplies — old pans for heating the wax or candle gel, utensils for stirring and cutting, even glass containers that caught my eye as attractive holders — at secondhand stores. Even the supplies you'll need to purchase, like wax and wicks, are fairly inexpensive. And lots of stuff, like cans for melting and molds of all shapes and sizes, comes right from the recycling bin! When using paraffin wax, your equipment will get pretty waxy and won't be much good to use for anything else, so be sure to ask permission before you use household items and containers that you find at home for your candle projects.

And before every candle-making project, please review my Ten Hot Safety Tips! on page 6.

Ten Hot Safety Tips!

A few of these tips are specifically for paraffin wax. For additional safety reminders about working with candle gel, see page 46.

1   **Always** have adult supervision and use pot holders when working with hot wax or gel.

2   **Never** leave melting wax or gel or a burning candle unattended!

3   **Don't** heat paraffin wax or gel over 200°F (93°C) and always use a thermometer when melting it to check the temperature. Wax doesn't boil like water but will keep heating until it reaches a flash point when it could catch fire.

4   **When** adding more wax (either solid or melted) to a container of melted wax, do it slowly and carefully so you don't splash the hot wax.

5   **Check** the amount of water in your melting pan frequently to make sure you always have enough (at least 2"/5 cm) in the bottom of the pan.

6   **If** you get hot paraffin wax on your hands, quickly dip them in cold water. The wax usually won't burn your skin and will peel off easily.

7   **Never** use water on a wax fire because wax floats on water. You can pour baking soda on a small fire or place the lid on your melting pan to smother any flames. But if you keep the temperature below 200°F (93°C) for both paraffin and gel so your wax melts slowly but safely, you shouldn't have trouble with wax fires.

8   **Always** cover your work area with newspaper and then with waxed paper. If any wax spills, let it harden and cool. Then just pull it off the waxed paper. You can remelt it and use it again.

9   **Be sure** to wear old clothes while working with wax.

10   **Never** pour hot paraffin wax down a drain; it will harden and clog the pipes. Save all extra melted wax in paper cups to be reused.

Basic Equipment

Most of these supplies are for molded (pages 19 to 35), dipped (page 36 to 43), and gel (pages 44 to 52) candles. For beeswax candles (pages 12 to 18), you only need sheets of beeswax and wicks.

CANDLE GEL. A new candle-making material. Although it isn't really a wax, I've included it under the discussion about waxes (Waxes, page 10).

CANS (all sizes). Metal cans for melting wax and gel and to make decorated holders; aluminum cans for molds. To keep colors pure, you'll need to melt each color in a separate can, so start saving clean, empty cans to have plenty on hand.

COLORING (crayons or candle dyes). I've found that good-quality crayons work just fine for coloring most candles. To make a light shade, add 1/8" (2.5 mm) of a crayon. The more color you add, the more opaque the candle will be. To get a nice uniform color throughout your candle, stir frequently to thoroughly mix the crayon with the hot wax and make sure the crayon is completely melted. (Some color may still settle at the bottom of the mold).

Real candle dyes (concentrated color cubes specifically for candle making) are best for hand-dipped (pages 36 to 43) and gel candles (pages 44 to 52).

CONTAINERS, plastic or cardboard. For molds for paraffin-wax candles. To collect simple, inexpensive molds, start in the kitchen! Small yogurt cups, milk cartons (all sizes), margarine or cottage cheese tubs, and ice cream, breadcrumb, and oatmeal containers all work well.

ELECTRIC BURNER. For melting wax and gel. An electric burner is safer, because a gas flame can ignite the materials if they get too hot. If you only have a gas stove at home, I strongly recommend buying a two-burner plug-in electric unit for your candle-making projects. Check thrift shops and yard sales for a secondhand one. For more safety tips on working with hot wax, see page 6; for gel, see page 46.

FRAGRANCE OILS. Special scents for candle making. Follow label directions for amounts needed — usually 3 to 4 drops per pound (500 g) of wax or gel is plenty. Too much scent can cause ripples in the top of the candle.

GLASS JARS. For containers for gel candles and as decorated holders for molded candles. Collect all shapes and sizes!

MOLD SEALER. A soft material like modeling clay for plugging small holes in molds where wax might leak out or for holding the wick tab in place.

NEWSPAPER. To cover your work area.

NONSTICK COOKING SPRAY. To coat molds so candles release easily.

PAN WITH LID. To place over the heat, holding the melting can set in a small amount of water. I melt both paraffin wax and candle gel this way, rather than directly over the heat. This safety precaution is so neither one gets too hot and ignites. The pan should be deep enough so you can cover it when the can is inside.

For more safety tips on working with hot wax or hot gel, see pages 6 and 46.

PAPER TOWELS. To wipe extra nonstick spray off the molds and to clean up your work area.

POT HOLDERS. To hold hot cans when pouring wax or gel.

SCISSORS. To cut wicks and molds and for crafting containers and candle decorations.

STEARINE. This wax additive helps candles burn longer, adds richer colors, and helps a molded candle release from the mold more easily.

THERMOMETER. An essential tool for making sure your melting wax or gel reaches the desired temperature without overheating to a dangerous level. Use a special thermometer for making candy and deep-frying (available at the grocery or hardware store or in a craft store with the candle-making supplies).

UTENSILS. Old butter knives, forks, and spoons for cutting and stirring wax and for smoothing and decorating candles. A spoon or chopstick works well for stirring melting wax. A metal spoon is best for stirring gel. (If you use a metal utensil, don't leave it sitting in the can.)

WAXED PAPER. To place over the newspaper covering your work area. Once any spilled wax dries, it will easily pull off the waxed paper and can be remelted.

WAXES. Waxes are available in many different forms with different melting points. But I use just three types — paraffin wax, beeswax, and candle gel — to create a wide variety of candle designs in all shapes and sizes, and in a range of vibrant colors (Waxes, page 10).

WICKS. Another very important item: Without a wick, your candle won't burn! See Wick Wise (page 11) to compare sizes and types.

WICK HOLDERS. Wrapping the top of the wick around a wick holder (which you lay across the top of the mold) keeps the wick centered as you pour the wax into the mold. Skewers, pencils, or chopsticks work well.

WICK TABS. Small metal tabs to weigh down the wick, holding it at the bottom of the candle. You can purchase wick tabs or use old bolts and washers.

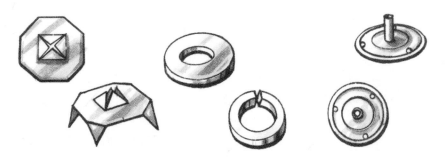

Waxes

Beeswax Sheets. Beeswax is sold in thin 8" x 16" (20 to 40 cm) sheets in natural or dyed colors in most craft stores. Beeswax sheets are easy and fun to use — rather than melting them, you roll them into the shapes you want! Beeswax also comes in blocks for melting, but they can be very expensive and they stick to molds easily. Plan on one sheet per candle.

Candle Gel. If you're a candle lover like me, you probably already own some gel candles. The good news is that this exciting candle-making material is readily available in craft stores and very easy to use, so now you can make your own gel candles (pages 44 to 52)! The gel comes in bags or in tubs (the package usually indicates how many candles it will make) and is available in brilliant colors. You pour the melted gel into a glass container. Rather than unmolding the candle, you burn it right in that holder.

Paraffin. Boxes of paraffin sticks can be found in most grocery and hardware stores in the baking section or with home-canning supplies. Paraffin is a medium melting-temperature wax (135° to 145°F/57° to 63°C) that works well for both molded (pages 19 to 35) and dipped (pages 36 to 43) candles. A one-pound (500 g) box of paraffin wax has four sticks. One stick yields ³/₄" cup (175 ml) of melted wax. You can use this to determine how much wax your particular mold or container will hold by first measuring how much water your mold or container can hold. It will hold the same amout of melted wax. Blocks of paraffin can be found in most craft stores, but they aren't as easy to work with because you have to cut them into smaller pieces before melting.

Wick Wise

The wick is the light source for your candle. Wicks are made from woven cotton threads and come in many sizes. The size wick you use depends on the size of your candle. If your wick is too thin, your candle flame will be small and will drown in the pool of melted wax. If your wick is too fat, it will burn too fast and be smoky. So when selecting a wick, keep in mind that the fatter the candle you're planning to make, the thicker the wick you will need.

   Prewaxed wicks are the easiest type to use for almost any type of candle, but in case you can't find them, or your mold calls for a longer wick than you can find prewaxed, I've given you some other choices.

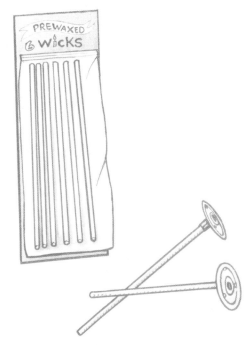

PREWAXED WICKS. These wicks have already been *primed* (dipped in melted wax) so they are ready to go right into the mold (Priming the Wick, page 22). Prewaxed wicks are especially handy for beeswax candles because you won't have melted wax for priming on hand. You may also see **prewaxed wire wicks**. The wire center (which burns off as the wick burns down) allows for a slower, more even burn. Some even come with the wick tabs (page 9) already attached.

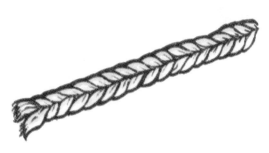

FLAT BRAIDED COTTON WICK. Comes in assorted sizes depending on the ply (the number of strands in the wick). The smaller the ply, the smaller the candle that wick should be used for. Best for dipped and beeswax candles but will work for molded candles, too.

SQUARE BRAIDED COTTON WICK. Best for molded candles.

Oh-So-Easy Beeswax Candles!

Beeswax candles are the simplest type of candle to make (no need to melt wax, just roll up a sheet of wax!), so they're a great place to start your candle-making adventures. Beeswax comes almost straight from the beehive [bees use up to 10 pounds (4.5 kg) of honey to make 1 pound (500 g) of combs!]. Even though the beeswax we buy in craft stores has been made into sheets for candle making, it still has a sticky feel and a honeycomb pattern and even smells like honey! These sheets come in their natural or assorted dyed colors, are quick and easy to use, and make very cool-looking candles that burn a long time. Long ago, beeswax candles were the favorite of kings and queens!

BASIC BEESWAX CANDLE

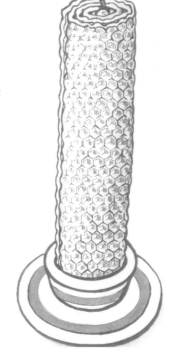

*B*eeswax comes in a variety of different sheet sizes. The wax sheets cut easily with scissors to create candles of different heights.

WHAT YOU NEED

Waxed paper
Prewaxed wick, cut to 6¹/₂" (16 cm)
Sheet of beeswax, 6" x 8" (15 x 20 cm)

WHAT YOU DO

1. **Set up your work area:** Gather your supplies so everything is handy before you start. Cover your work area with waxed paper.

2. **Create your candle:** Place the wick on the shorter edge of the beeswax sheet and gently press it into place.

Slowly roll the entire sheet of wax around the wick.

Press the bottom of the candle against a flat surface to flatten the bottom so the candle stands up straight and sits securely. Presto! A sweet-smelling beeswax candle!

A Gallery of Special Effects!

*C*reate awesome designs and patterns on your beeswax candles! Beeswax sheets can be torn or broken into smaller pieces easily with your hands or cut with scissors.

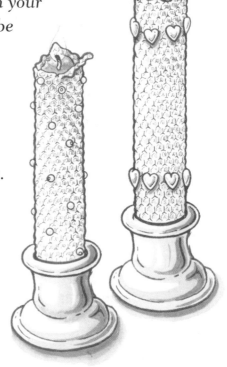

Jazz it up!

Press in beads or jewels.

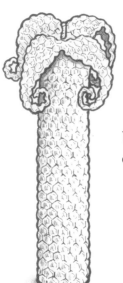

Zigzag it!

Before you roll, cut the top edge of the beeswax sheet in a zigzag design.

Once the candle is rolled, curl the points down.

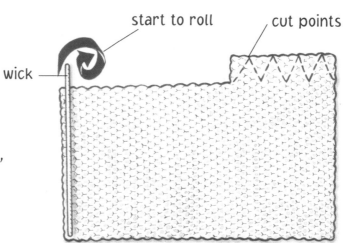

start to roll

cut points

wick

Trim it!

Gently press small pieces of different-colored beeswax onto the finished candle.

wick

flare this edge

Spiral it!

Cut the beeswax sheet at an angle. Place the wick along the longest edge and slowly roll. Flare the outside edge as you roll, then smooth it with your finger.

TRICKS OF THE TRADE

Oops! A wax spill

To safely clean up a paraffin wax spill on a carpet or candle drippings on a tablecloth, use a brown paper bag as a blotter. Place it over the spilled wax then (with adult help) run a hot iron over it. The bag will absorb most of the wax. Or, after the wax has hardened on the fabric, rub with an ice cube and the wax should be easy to peel off.

Beehive Candle

A *mini-beehive, complete with wax "bees"!*

WHAT YOU NEED

Waxed paper
Prewaxed wick, cut to 6½" (16 cm)
Sheet of natural-color beeswax,
   6" x 8" (15 x 20 cm)
Small pieces of beeswax, in a dark
   or contrasting color
Scissors

WHAT YOU DO

1. **Set up your work area:** Gather your supplies so
   everything is handy before you start. Cover your work
   area with waxed paper.

2. **Create your candle:** Cut the sheet in half lengthwise on
   a slight angle. Rotate the top half and place it on the
   bottom half as shown.

Place the wick on the taller edge of the beeswax piece and gently press it into place.

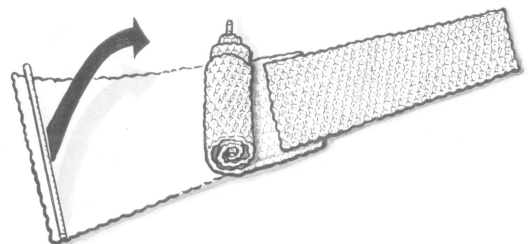

As you roll, press the outside edges in to create the beehive shape.

Press the bottom of the candle against a flat surface so it will stand up straight and sit securely.

3. From the smaller pieces of beeswax, form "bees." Press them onto the hive.

Working with Beeswax

If your wax sheets are cold and brittle, place them on a cookie sheet in an unheated oven. It will be just warm enough in there to soften them slightly. As you work with the beeswax, the warmth from your hands will soften it more and it will get easier to work with.

Beeswax Buddies

Beeswax sheets don't always have to be rolled. For truly one-of-a-kind beeswax candles, use pieces of beeswax to create figures or your favorite animals!

WHAT YOU NEED

Waxed paper
Sheets or scraps of beeswax, in
    assorted colors
Skewer
Prewaxed wicks
Scissors

WHAT YOU DO

1. Shape and sculpt a figure or animal from the beeswax. Use smaller bits and pieces to decorate it.

2. With the skewer, poke a hole in the top of the candle. Insert a prewaxed wick and trim it to fit, leaving a 1/2" (1 cm) wick.

Many Marvelous Molded Candles

A molded candle — where you create a shape by pouring melted wax into a container, let it harden, and then remove the container — is the most versatile method of candle making. The shapes, colors, and decorations you can create are almost endless! Some of my favorite molds are the simplest. A cardboard milk or juice carton with the top opened up completely is perfect for an ice candle (pages 28 to 29), for example.

Some molds are reusable, and others are disposable (you will have to destroy them to get your candle out). So take a look around and be creative. Just remember that whatever you pour wax into may not be able to be used again or come completely clean so be sure to ask first (and stay away from the good china!). And always test a new material with a small amount of hot wax first.

BASIC MOLDED CANDLE

With these instructions, you can make candles of many different shapes, sizes, and colors. Once you feel comfortable with the basic process of making a molded candle, try some of the variations, such as layered (pages 26 to 27) or stacked (page 32) candles, as well as the decorating ideas (pages 34 to 35). If you need to review the supplies, see pages 7 to 9.

WHAT YOU NEED

Newspaper
Waxed paper
Pan with lid
Melting can
Electric burner
Paraffin wax (please ask an adult to help you melt and pour the wax)
Candy/deep-fry thermometer
Clean, dry container for mold
Nonstick cooking spray
Paper towels
Wick
Wick tab
Wick holder
Scissors
Stirring stick
Stearine
Fragrance oil, optional
Color (crayons or candle dye), optional
Pot holders
Butter knife, optional

TRICKS OF THE TRADE
Faster melting

Wax sticks melt faster when cut into cubes. For easy cutting, dip a butter knife in the hot water from your melting pan. The knife heats up just enough to cut through the sticks easily and safely.

WHAT YOU DO

1. **Set up your work area:** Gather all your supplies so everything is handy before you start. Cover your work area with newspaper and then waxed paper for easy cleanup of wax spills. Fill the pan with at least 2" (5 cm) of water (and have more water close by to add if necessary). Set the melting can in the water and place the pan on the burner; cover the pan.

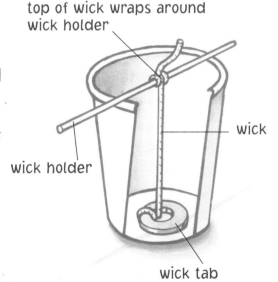

2. **Begin melting the wax:** Melt the wax over medium heat, checking the temperature with the thermometer frequently.

3. **Prepare the mold:** Coat the inside of the mold evenly with a small amount of nonstick cooking spray. Wipe off any extra with the paper towels.

4. **Prepare the wick:** If using an unwaxed cotton wick, prime it (page 22). Tie the wick tab to the bottom of the wick. Holding the wick in the center of the mold; wrap it around the wick holder. Cut to fit if necessary. Tie the top of the wick to the wick holder.

top of wick wraps around
wick holder

wick

wick holder

wick tab

5. **Prepare the wax:** Stir and check the temperature of the wax. When the wax is completely melted, add stearine (use amount directed on package) and stir. Add a couple of drops of fragrance oil, if desired. Add color. Stir until completely mixed.

leave ½" (1 cm) at the
top rim of the mold

6. **Create your candle:** Using pot holders, carefully pour the melted wax into the mold as shown. Save a small amount of melted wax to top it off later. Let set about one hour, or until completely hardened.

7. **Topping off:** As your candle cools, the wax may "dip" in the center. After the candle has hardened and before you remove the mold, pour the melted wax evenly over the top of the candle to fill the indent around the wick.

Priming the Wick

COTTON WICKS BURN BEST when they have been primed (coated in wax). It helps them to light better and to burn with a stronger flame. Keeping your fingers away from the hot melted wax, dip the wick in and out (don't worry about priming the tip that you're holding), straighten it, and place it on a piece of waxed paper for a few minutes. Then dip again and let dry. Now your wick is ready for candle making. If you buy waxed wicks, you won't need to prime them.

8. Remove the mold: Remove the wick holder. Gently pull the mold away from the hardened wax. Letting in a little air makes it easier to pop the candle out of the mold. Pull on the wick gently, if necessary. Trim the wick to about 1/2" (1 cm).

If using a cardboard or plastic mold, gently peel or cut it away from the candle.

With the butter knife, "shave" the top edge of the candle to smooth it out, if necessary.

MORE
MOLDED-CANDLE FUN!

TRY A FOIL MOLD! Even a piece of aluminum foil can be a mold. It is very easy to remove from the candle, and the crumpled foil gives the outside of the candle an interesting texture. A foil mold is best for small, low candles. Use a double layer of heavy-duty foil and be sure the sides of the foil are at least 2" (5 cm) higher than the height of the melted wax.

PILLAR CANDLE

n ot all wicks will be at the top of your mold — sometimes candles are made upside down! An aluminum can is the perfect mold for the tall, thick candles you see in candle shops, called pillars. It is just the right size and shape, and the shape of the bottom creates a nice rim around the top of the candle.

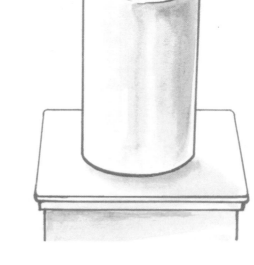

WHAT YOU NEED

Supplies for the Basic
   Molded Candle (page 20)
Scissors or sharp knife
   (for use by an adult)
Aluminum can
Masking tape
Mold sealer

WHAT YOU DO

1. **Follow steps 1 and 2** of the Basic Molded Candle (page 21).

2. **Ask an adult to make the mold:** Cut the top off the aluminum can by inserting the knife or one point of the scissors in the can near the top and cutting completely around.

The edge will be sharp, so cover it with a piece of tape around the top. Poke a hole just big enough for the wick in the center of the bottom of the can.

Evenly coat the inside of the can with the nonstick spray. Wipe off any extra with the paper towels.

3. **Prepare the wick:** Pull the wick through the hole from the outside to the inside, leaving 1/2" (1 cm) for the wick end. Seal the hole with mold sealer. Tape the wick if necessary to lie flat.

Wind the other end of the wick around the wick holder at the top of the can (which will actually be the bottom of your candle).

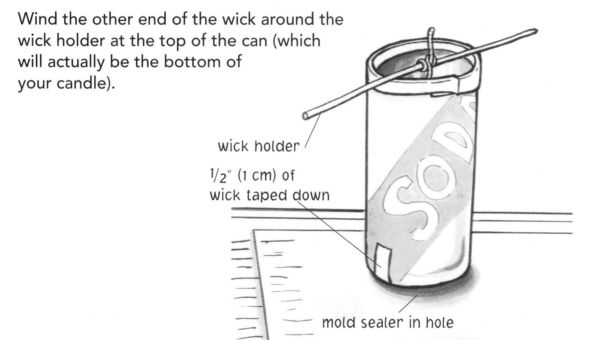

wick holder

1/2" (1 cm) of wick taped down

mold sealer in hole

4. **Follow steps 5 through 7** of the Basic Molded Candle (page 22). Let the candle dry about four to six hours. No topping off necessary! When removing the mold, first remove the tape from the top of the wick, then gently pull the candle out. Trim the wick at the bottom and "shave" it smooth with the butter knife, if necessary.

LAYERED CANDLE

Create amazing color combos by layering different colors of wax. The layers can be thin and close together or thick to create bold stripes — or a combination of both! A layered candle takes some time to make, because each different color has to set before you pour on the next one, but it is worth the wait!

WHAT YOU NEED

Supplies for the Basic Molded Candle (page 20)

WHAT YOU DO

1. **Follow steps 1 through 5** of the Basic Molded Candle (pages 21 to 22), melting each color in a separate can. So that the wax for the next layer doesn't set while you're waiting for the poured layer to set, melt one color at a time.

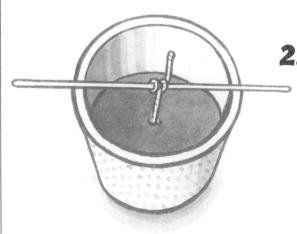

2. Using the pot holders, slowly pour the desired amount of melted wax for one layer. Let stand until the wax has formed a solid crust. The standing time for each layer depends on how thick it is. Thin layers only need to set about 20 minutes; thicker layers need about 40 minutes.

3. Melt another color of wax and repeat step 2. Melt and pour until you have as many layers as you want, leaving about ½" (1 cm) at the top rim of the mold. Remember to save a little of the final color for topping off (page 22, step 7). Let the finished candle set about one hour, or until completely hardened.

4. To remove the mold, follow step 8 of the Basic Molded Candle (page 23).

TRICKS OF THE TRADE
Layers separating?

If the layers of your candle come apart once it's removed from the mold, you may be letting the layers stand too long. Next time, use a metal skewer to poke two or three holes in each layer before pouring in the next color. Some of the hot wax will flow into the holes so the layers will be attached to each other!

MORE
LAYERED-CANDLE FUN!

TO CREATE SLANTED LAYERS, place your mold in a bowl of sand so the wax dries at an angle. Change the angle for each layer. (A finished slanted layer candle is on page 19.)

ICE-CAVERN CANDLE

Here's an all-time favorite! Ice candles are very delicate and intricate. It's fascinating to watch the hot wax instantly take shape around the freezing ice, creating unique caverns and mazes.

WHAT YOU NEED

Supplies for the Basic
    Molded Candle (page 20)
Metal skewer
Tape
Mold sealer
Crushed ice

WHAT YOU DO

1. **Follow steps 1 and 2** of Basic Molded Candle (page 21), using half as much paraffin wax as the container will hold to allow room for the ice. (Cardboard cartons that peel off easily work best for this candle.)

2. **Prepare the wick:** Prime the wick (page 22), if necessary. With the skewer, poke a hole in the center of the bottom of the container and pull about 3/4" (2 cm) of the wick through. Tape the wick flat and seal the hole with mold sealer.

wick

tape

3. Center and secure the wick in the container with the wick holder.

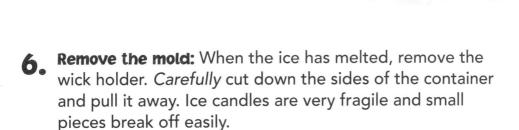

4. **Follow step 5** of the Basic Molded Candle (page 22).

5. Fill the container with crushed ice. Using pot holders, slowly pour the wax over the crushed ice. The wax will harden instantly.

6. **Remove the mold:** When the ice has melted, remove the wick holder. *Carefully* cut down the sides of the container and pull it away. Ice candles are very fragile and small pieces break off easily.

TRICKS OF THE TRADE
Storing candles

Always store candles away from direct sunlight and heat. Direct sunlight will fade the candle colors and heat will start to melt them, causing them to lose their shape.

MORE
ICE-CANDLE FUN!

ADDING GLITTER TO THE MELTED WAX works especially well with ice candles. The wax sets instantly (before the glitter settles at the bottom of the mold).

POUR TWO COLORS OF MELTED WAX into the mold at the same time.

Round Candles!

To make a round candle, follow the instructions for the Basic Molded Candle (pages 20 to 23) using a round mold from a craft or candle-supply store. Follow the instructions that came with the mold to release the candle.

A squeeze of red quickly turns this round candle into a baseball!

Create an amazing mosaic design with small pieces of beeswax.

SMALL SHAPED CANDLES

Use these small candles individually — they make great floating candles and cake toppers! — or stack them (page 32). Make extras for decorating other candles (Pot of Roses Candle, pages 56 to 57).

WHAT YOU NEED

Supplies for the Basic Molded
  Candle (page 20)
Shaped molds, such as decorative
  ice-cube trays or soap molds
Skewer

WHAT YOU DO

1. **Follow steps 1 through 6** for the Basic Molded Candle (pages 21 to 22). When you get to step 4, prime the wick if necessary but don't secure it in the mold. With these small candles, you insert the wick after the candle hardens. They harden in about an hour.

2. To remove the wax shapes from the mold, you pop them out just like ice cubes. Breaking away the *side* of the wax from the tray lets in an air pocket.

3. Once the candles are out of the molds, use the skewer to poke holes through the center of each shape. Pull the wick through and cut it off about 1/2" (1 cm) above the top of the candle.

MORE
SHAPED-CANDLE FUN!

STACK THEM! Small shaped candles look really cool stacked to create a taller candle. For this design, you'll need different-sized molds of the same shape. Start with the largest shape on the bottom and just keep pulling the wick through to stack several candles. Trim the wick about 1/2" (1 cm) from the top of the candle.

COOKIE-CUTTER CANDLES

Bunnies, reindeer, bells, stars — any shape you can find in a cookie cutter can be a candle!

WHAT YOU NEED

Supplies for the Basic Molded
   Candle (page 20)
Plastic food trays (from fruits or
   vegetables only)
Cookie cutters
Skewer

WHAT YOU DO

1. **Follow steps 1 through 5** of the Basic Molded Candle (pages 21 to 22) to melt several colors of wax. When you get to step 4, just prime the wick if necessary. With these small candles, you insert the wick after the candle hardens.

2. Using pot holders, carefully pour the melted wax into the plastic trays. Making sure the trays are level, let the wax set for about 40 minutes.

3. Before the wax hardens completely, press each cookie cutter into it, then gently pull it out with the wax shape in it.

4. Let the shapes dry completely, then push them out of the cutters.

5. With the skewer, poke holes in the center of each shape. Pull the wick through and cut it off about 1/2" (1 cm) above the top of the candle.

MORE
COOKIE-CUTTER FUN!

YOUR NAME IN LIGHTS! Use alphabet cookie cutters to make individual letters. Use the skewer to add several wicks and light up any name. Great as a cake topper!

CREATE CANDLE PEOPLE! Use a gingerbread man or woman cookie cutter to make a standing candle. Shape small "shoes" out of modeling clay around the feet so the candle will stand securely. This makes a great gift when you use acrylic paint to decorate it so it resembles the recipient!

A Gallery of Special Effects

Now that you've learned the basics of candle making, let the fun begin! There are so many ways to decorate and enhance your candles, making each one a unique creation and a reflection of your own personal taste. And be sure to check out the Cool Candleholders (pages 53 to 62).

Filled with surprises!

Add a whole new look to a Basic Molded Candle (pages 20 to 23) by filling the mold with pretty or fun-looking objects! Choose objects that won't burn, like beads, pebbles, marbles, shells, metal charms, or tiny erasers. Or use chunks (below) of a different-colored wax.

Pour a little wax into the bottom of the mold. Let it sit until the wax thickens, then press the objects into place against the sides. Fill the rest of the way and let harden completely.

A layer of cool blue wax, topped with shells and clear wax. Now if only you could add the scent of suntan lotion!

To use chunks, fill the container with the chunks and pour the melted wax over them.

Glue on shapes

Use white craft glue to glue Small Shaped Candles (page 31) on the outside of a larger candle. For this sea horse candle, I used a soap mold. Top off with a small pool of the same-colored wax, if you like.

To help the glue adhere better, score the wax first by scratching the candle surface with a fork or toothpick.

Paint it!

You can paint on any candle. There are paints sold especially for candles in craft stores or you can use acrylics. I really like using squeeze-bottle paints — it makes decorating *so* fun and easy!

Traditional Hand-Dipped Candles

Hand dipping is the traditional way of making candles. The earliest candles made were essential for indoor light, so they were made to fit chandeliers, sconces (wall candleholders), and candlesticks. To create hand-dipped candles, also called tapers, you continually dip a wick in hot wax. As each layer hardens, the candle gets thicker. So take a step back in time and rediscover this age-old craft!

BASIC HAND-DIPPED CANDLE

It takes about 10 dips for a thin taper and between 25 to 30 dips for a standard-sized taper. Tiny tapers are delicate and pretty. If you are the patient type, try making a larger, thicker one.

WHAT YOU NEED

Newspaper
Waxed paper
Pan with lid
Deep melting can (candle will only be
   as tall as the melting can)
Electric burner
Paraffin wax (ask for adult help to melt and pour)
Candy/deep-fry thermometer
Flat braided cotton wick
Ruler
Scissors
Stearine
Color (candle dye), optional
Fragrance oil, optional
Stirring stick
Can of cool water
Paper towels
Box to hold cooling candles (deeper than the length of your candles)

WHAT YOU DO

1. **Set up your work area:** Gather all your supplies so everything is handy before you start. Cover your work area with newspaper and then waxed paper for easy cleanup of wax spills. Fill the pan with at least 2" (5 cm) of water (and have more water close by to add if necessary). Set the melting can in the water and place the pan on the burner; cover the pan.

2. **Begin melting the wax:** Melt the wax over medium heat, checking the temperature with the thermometer frequently. Melt enough wax to fill the can about 1" (2.5 cm) from top.

3. **Prepare the wick:** To make two dipped candles at a time, decide how tall you would like the candles to be (remember, they will only be as tall as your melting can). Then cut the wick so it's twice that height, plus about 3" (7.5 cm) extra. Now you can hold the wick in the center and as the candles get thicker, they won't stick together.

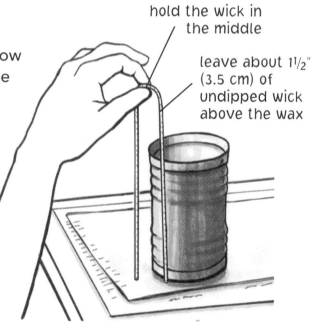

hold the wick in the middle

leave about 1½" (3.5 cm) of undipped wick above the wax

4. **Prepare the wax:** Add stearine, color, and fragrance oil (if you like) to the melted wax. Let the color melt; stir thoroughly. Check the temperature again (Wax Temperatures, page 40).

5. **Create your candles:** Dip both ends of the wick into the melting can, dipping evenly and bringing them out slowly. Pull the wicks down gently at the bottoms to straighten them. Or, you can roll them on waxed paper in between dips to smooth out any lumps.

Dip the candle in a can of cool water between wax dips. Pat with the paper towels before dipping back in the hot wax again.

Continue to dip until desired candle thickness is reached, straightening and cooling the wick between each dip. As you use up the wax, you may need to add more to the melting can to keep the level the same as the length of your candle.

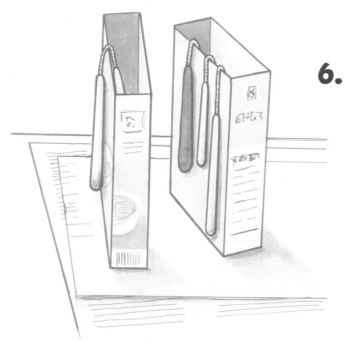

6. **Dry the candles:** Hang the candles to dry over the sides of the box for about an hour. After they harden, cut the unwaxed wick in the center so you have two candles. Trim each wick to about 1/2" (1 cm).

Or, while the candles are still warm, see A Gallery of Special Effects (pages 42 to 43) for some fun decorations.

Wax Temperatures

FOR BEST RESULTS with tapers, the paraffin wax should be between 125°F to 150°F (52°C to 66°C). If the bottom of your candle is too thin, your wax is too hot and it's melting the wax of the previous layer. If your candle is lumpy, your wax is too cool.

RAINBOW DIPPED CANDLE

Slender and graceful, with delicate shades of color, the rainbow candle is one of my favorites!

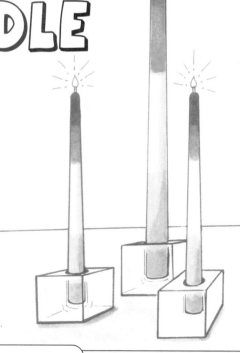

WHAT YOU NEED

Supplies for the Basic Hand-Dipped Candle (page 37)
Color (candle dye), in yellow, red, and blue

WHAT YOU DO

1. **Follow the steps** for the Basic Dipped Candle (pages 38 to 39) to create one yellow candle.

2. Dip the top third of your candle in red, this will give you an orange layer first. Then dip just 1" (2.5 cm) of the tip in again to get a paler red shade.

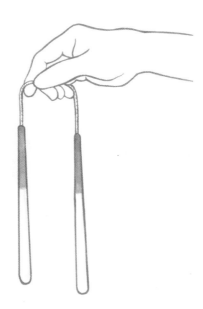

3. Dip the bottom third of your candle in blue to make a green layer. Then dip the bottom 1" (2.5 cm) again to get a more opaque blue color.

TRICKS OF THE TRADE
Nice and smooth!

Use an old nylon stocking or panty hose to smooth over any nicks and scrapes in your candle once it is completely dry.

A Gallery of Special Effects!

While dipped candles are still warm, they can be shaped, twisted, and braided easily. You can also paint your candles once they've cooled. Look for special candle-decorating "paint" (it's actually liquid wax) in fine-tip tubes.

Go for a zigzag!

Place candles on waxed paper. Twist around a skewer; pull away from skewer when hardened.

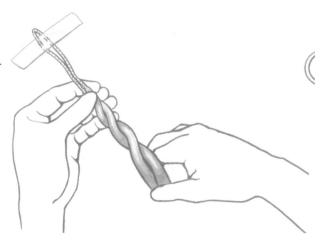

Do the twist

Twist two thin tapers together. Press the wicks together at the top to make one.

Braid them!

Using three tapers of equal size, hold the wicks together with a clothespin and braid the tapers together. Press the wicks together at the top to make one.

Bend them!

How many interesting shapes can you make?

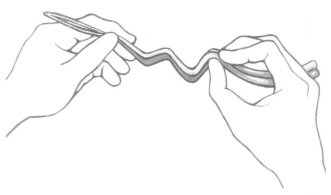

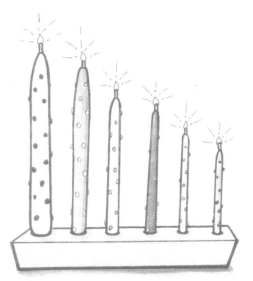

Paint them!

Tiny dots of paint in a contrasting color will jazz up your tapers.

Decorating with Tapers

TO MAKE MINI-HOLDERS for thin tapers, shape a small piece of still-warm wax into a base and poke in a skewer to make a hole. Or, decorate empty wooden thread spools with paint, beads, or glitter.

WINEGLASSES WITH WIDE STEMS make elegant holders for small tapers. Paint a design on the outside of glass if you like. Cut the taper so the flame will be even with the top rim of glass, and use a bit of clay at the base to secure it. Looks awesome!

Brilliant Gel Candles

Gel candles are fairly new to the candle world, but they have quickly become very popular. To make gel candles, you melt a jelly-like product and pour it directly into the decorative container in which you will display your candle (rather than into a mold). The gel isn't sticky like wax and it peels easily off surfaces, so pans and containers can be washed and reused.

Candle gel is available in a wide variety of bright colors (or you can color it yourself), so you can create awesome layered designs. And it's transparent, so you can see right through your gel candles! This makes designing with beads, charms, and other decorations even more fun.

Working with Candle Gel

Before you start, review the list of candle-making supplies (pages 7 to 9). Candle gel is a somewhat new material, so here are a few additional reminders.

- **ALTHOUGH YOU CAN BUY** clear gel and dye it yourself, I always purchase tinted gel because it comes in such awesome colors. If you do color the gel yourself, be sure to use real candle dye (follow the instructions on the package for the amount). Crayons will make your gel candles more opaque.

- **USE ONLY A FEW DROPS** of fragrance oil for gel candles; adding too much can be a fire hazard.

- **USE GLASS CONTAINERS** so you can see the beautiful colors and designs. In a very tall container, like the one I used for the Layered Gel Candle (pages 50 to 51), the wick tends to drift when you pour in the gel, so a little bit of mold sealer (page 8) is a good idea to hold it in place. Mold sealer can cause extra bubbles in gel, however, so I don't recommend using it for most gel candles.

- **WHEN YOU HEAT THE GEL,** stir it with a metal spoon (it will cause fewer bubbles to form than a wooden spoon or stirring stick).

- **PREWAXED WICKS ARE IDEAL** for gel candles because you don't have to prime them (Priming the Wick, page 22).

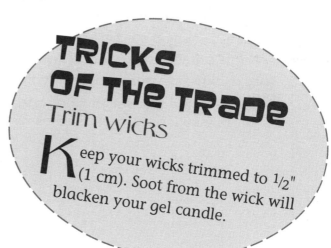

TRICKS OF THE TRADE

Trim wicks

Keep your wicks trimmed to 1/2" (1 cm). Soot from the wick will blacken your gel candle.

Six Hot Safety Tips!

1   **Always** have adult supervision and use pot holders when working around the hot candle gel.

2   **The instructions** on the container of candle gel may indicate that you can melt it in a pan over direct heat, but it is actually *more* flammable than paraffin wax, so I don't recommend that. I melt it in a can set in a covered pan of water on an electric burner.

3   **Melt** the gel slowly over low heat and use a candy/deep-fry thermometer to check the temperature frequently. Never heat the gel above the temperature indicated on the package. High temperatures are a fire hazard.

4   **After** pouring the gel into the mold, wipe up any drips with the paper towels. If small pieces of gel get on stove burners, they will make a lot of smoke as they burn off.

5   **If** you get hot gel on your skin, quickly submerge the area in cold water and then peel the gel off. Candle gel doesn't cool down as quickly as melted wax and although you won't get an actual burn, you will feel the heat a little longer.

6   **Gel** has mineral oil in it and can leave oil stains on fabric and carpets. Protect your work area with waxed paper. Watch out for little crumbs of gel as you work and clean them up right away.

BASIC GEL CANDLE

*O*nce you see how easy the basic gel candle is, you'll be ready to move right on to the real fun — designing and decorating!

WHAT YOU NEED

Newspaper
Waxed paper
Pan with lid
Electric burner
Melting can
Metal spoon
Candle gel, clear or colored
   (please ask an adult to help
   you melt and pour the gel)
Candy/deep-fry thermometer

Scissors
Prewaxed wick
Glass container
Wick tab
Tape or mold sealer
Wick holder
Candle dye (if coloring the clear gel)
Fragrance oil, optional
Pot holders

WHAT YOU DO

1. **Set up your work area:** Gather all your supplies so everything is handy before you start. Cover your work surface with newspaper and then waxed paper for easy cleanup of any spills.

   Fill the pan with about 2" (5 cm) of water (and make sure you have more water handy). Set the pan on the burner and place the melting can in the pan; cover the pan.

2. **Heat the gel:** Spoon the gel into the melting can, being careful not to drop gel crumbs. Melt the gel over *low* heat to the temperature recommended on the package, checking the temperature frequently with the thermometer.

TRICKS OF THE TRADE
Keep an eye on the wick

Pour slowly, watching the wick as you pour the gel into the container to make sure it is staying centered. Wicks tend to drift a little even when weighted.

3. **Prepare the wick:** Cut the wick to the height of the container, plus an extra inch (cm) or so. Tie a wick tab to the bottom of the wick; secure the tab with a piece of tape or a little mold sealer. Center the wick in the container; secure it by wrapping the top once or twice around the wick holder.

wick

wick holder

wick tab

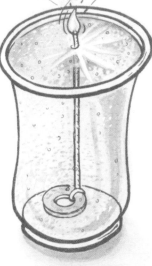

TRICKS OF THE TRADE
Use your noodle!

As your candle burns down, the wick will get lower in the container. To light a hard-to-reach wick, light a spaghetti noodle and use it like a match.

4. **Prepare the gel:** When the gel is liquid, stir in the candle dye and fragrance oil, if using.

5. **Create your candle:** Using pot holders, carefully pour the hot gel into the container, leaving about 1/2" (1 cm) of space at the top. The more slowly you pour, the fewer air bubbles you will create.

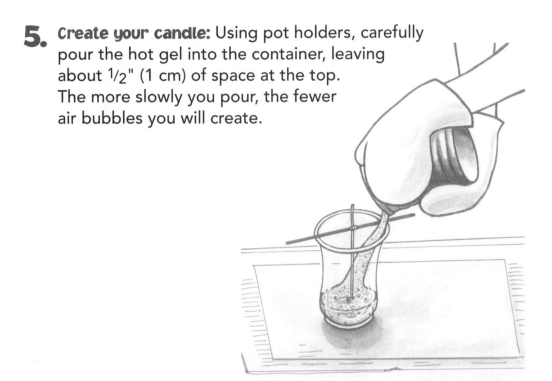

6. **Let it cool:** Set the container in a place where it won't be disturbed. Let the gel cool about an hour. Remove the wick holder and trim the wick to 1/2" (1 cm).

Don't mind the bubbles!

BUBBLES WILL ALMOST ALWAYS show up in your gel candles. To create the least amount, try pouring the gel at an angle (and pour slowly). Or, place your candle in the refrigerator to cool. (Use a pot holder — the container may still be very hot!). Using glue to hold decorative items in place will also cause extra bubbles. Don't worry about it too much — bubbles are part of the look of a gel candle. Most of the time, they look nice and add to the character of the candle.

LAYERED GEL CANDLE

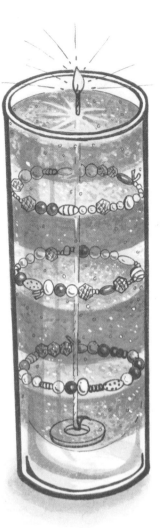

Layers of different-colored gel make a spectacular candle! I particularly like the look of layers of colored gel alternating with layers of clear gel. Add beads in complementary colors if you like. For this design, I strung beads and tiny charms on colored craft wire and decorated the clear layers with these mini "bracelets."

WHAT YOU NEED

Craft wire and beads, optional
Supplies for the Basic Gel Candle
    (page 47)
Tall narrow glass container
Candle gel, clear and two colors
    (please ask an adult to help you
    melt and pour the gel)
Butter knife or chopstick

WHAT YOU DO

1. **Make the bracelets, if using:** Cut a piece of craft wire that fits around the inside of the container with a little extra at each end. Cut two more pieces of wire the same length. String on beads to almost fill each wire; twist the ends together to form the bracelets.

2. **Follow steps 1 through 4** for the Basic Gel Candle (pages 47 to 49), preparing clear and two colors of gel. Use the knife or chopstick to center the wick tab.

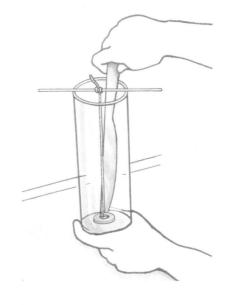

3. **Create your candle:** Using the pot holders, carefully pour in a layer of clear gel; let set about 10 minutes. Add a bracelet, if using. The knife or chopstick is handy for positioning the bracelet in the gel.

Pour in a layer of the first color; let set. Pour in the second color; let set. Repeat the sequence, letting each layer set so the colors don't blend and the bracelets stay where you place them, until you have filled the container.

4. **Let it cool:** Set the container in a place where it won't be disturbed. Let the gel cool about an hour. Remove the wick holder and trim the wick to about 1/2" (1 cm).

MORE
GEL-CANDLE FUN!

BITS OF COLORED WIRE, metal charms, miniature ceramic or glass figures, coins, marbles, glitter, sand, shells, and pebbles can all be added to gel candles for decoration. Be sure to play it safe: Don't use any objects that would burn or melt.

CUT CHUNKS OR CUBES OF SOLID GEL and use them as decorations in melted gel of a contrasting color.

SEASHELL GEL CANDLE

C reate a tropical paradise in a glass! I live on an island, so many of my candles have a "beach" theme, with sand and shells as decorations. This is one of my favorite designs!

WHAT YOU NEED

Supplies for the Basic Gel
   Candle (page 47)
Candle gel, clear or pale blue
   (please ask an adult to help
   you melt and pour the gel)
Candle dye, blue
   (if coloring the clear gel)
Sand
Shells

WHAT YOU DO

1. **Follow steps 1 through 4** of the Basic Gel Candle (pages 47 to 49).

2. **Create your candle:** Spread a layer of sand in the bottom of the container. Pour about 1/2" (1 cm) of gel over the sand and let cool a few minutes. Place shells in the gel as it cools, close to the glass.

   After the first gel layer has set, fill the container with melted gel.

3. **Let it cool:** Set the container in a place where it won't be disturbed. Let the gel cool about an hour. Remove the wick holder and trim the wick to about 1/2" (1 cm).

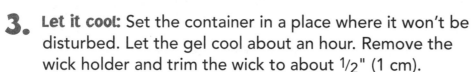

Cool Candleholders

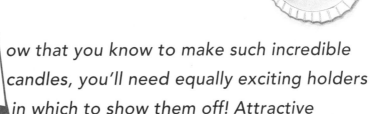

Now that you know to make such incredible candles, you'll need equally exciting holders in which to show them off! Attractive candleholders can be made from a wide assortment of inexpensive containers as long as they are safe and nonflammable. Small glass jars and flower vases are easy to decorate and are perfect for displaying all sizes and shapes of handmade candles. Depending upon the materials you're working with, you can also create the candle right in the decorative container. Terra-cotta pots and seashells, for example, are great molds for wax candles. Here are some of my favorite ways to display candles at home and present them as gifts.

DECORATED GLASS HOLDERS

Take a look at the glass jars in your kitchen — you'll be amazed at the variety of sizes and shapes they come in. Also, keep an eye out for small glass flower vases at thrift shops and yard sales. Even the simplest container can be turned into a fantastic candleholder with just a few decorations!

Here I used strips of tissue paper, but you could also use acrylic paints. Top the rim with a strip of beaded fringe, then glue on a piece of decorative ribbon in matching colors.

Get creative with beads, glitter, and glue!

Jazz up a simple white candle in a glass jar by gluing on different colors of embroidery thread.

DECORATED EGGSHELL HOLDER

I've always loved decorating eggs, so I was delighted to discover they make beautiful candleholders. I display them in painted sections of a cardboard egg carton, either singly or several sections together.

WHAT YOU NEED

Egg(s)
Empty egg carton
Decorations: egg dyes (follow instructions on package), acrylic paints in squeeze tubes, tissue paper, glitter, sequins, glue
Supplies for the Basic Molded Candle (page 20)
Skewer

1. Carefully crack just the top of the egg and peel off the cracked shell. Empty the egg out (refrigerate for cooking). Rinse out the shell and set it in the egg carton to dry. Wash your hands when you are finished handling the raw egg.

2. Dye the egg first, if you like, following the instructions on the package of egg dye.

3. Set the eggshell in the egg carton. Using the eggshell as the mold, follow the steps for the Basic Molded Candle (pages 21 to 22). You won't need to coat the inside of the egg or set up the wick.

4. Decorate the shell as desired (Tricks of the Trade, (page 57).

MORE
SHELL-CONTAINER FUN!

BEACH LOVER'S DELIGHT! Seashells are beautiful molds for small candles.

POT OF ROSES CANDLE

Terra-cotta pots come in many different sizes and can be found at most garden stores. They make great candle molds! These pots are made from unglazed clay so you'll need to paint them first on the outside to seal the clay and protect your surface from waxy splotches. Try a decorated pot of pink wax roses set in green wax — especially nice as a scented candle!

WHAT YOU NEED

Acrylic paints and small paintbrushes
Small terra-cotta pot
Supplies for the Basic Molded Candle (page 20),
    including green coloring
Pink wax flowers, 4 (Small Shaped Candles, page 31)

WHAT YOU DO

1. Paint the outside (and the inside rim, too, if you like) of the terra-cotta pot; let dry.

2. Fill the drain hole with the mold sealer.

3. Follow steps 1 through 6 of the Basic Molded Candle (pages 21 to 22). Let the wax harden slightly. Then remove the wick holder and set the wax flowers around the wick. Let harden. Trim the wick to about 1/2" (1 cm).

MORE
TERRA-COTTA POT FUN!

LOTS OF DOTS! Use 3-D "dots" of paint to create cool designs.

A "CHARMING" GIFT! Spell out a friend's name by stringing her name or initials on craft wire around the pot. A perfect party favor!

TRICKS OF THE TRADE
Handy egg holders

Place the eggshell over one finger to decorate. A chopstick or pencil set in a container of sand or secured with a bit of modeling clay makes a handy drying rack. Or, poke a chopstick through a section of the egg carton and set the eggshell over it.

DELICATE WAX BOWL

H ow about a delicate handmade wax bowl to hold your handmade candle? Dried flowers or small shells look especially pretty pressed into the sides. Or, decorate your bowl with different-colored wax dribbles! For a magical look, fill it with water and float two or three of the shaped candles (page 31) in it. If you like this design, check out the Hurricane Candle (pages 60 to 61).

WHAT YOU NEED

Supplies for the Basic Molded
    Candle (page 20)
Small paper bowl for mold
Decorations, optional

WHAT YOU DO

1. **Follow steps 1 through 6** of the Basic Molded Candle (pages 21 to 22). Let cool 20 to 30 minutes.

2. When you see the wax starting to dry around the edges, carefully scoop out the soft wax in the middle, leaving walls about 1/2" (1 cm) thick.

3. **For a plain bowl:** Smooth the inside of the wax bowl with the butter knife or your finger (the wax will be warm but not too hot to touch and the wax will peel right off your fingers).

For a decorated bowl: From the inside, carefully press decorations all the way into the wax wall, then smooth over those spots with your finger.

Let the bowl dry completely.

4. To remove the mold, tear away the bowl.

MORE
WAX-BOWL FUN!

ONCE THE BOWL IS OUT OF THE MOLD, place it upside down over an empty can. Using pot holders, pour a small amount of melted wax into a small paper cup, pinch the edge to form a spout and dribble the wax over the bowl. Decorate with different colors.

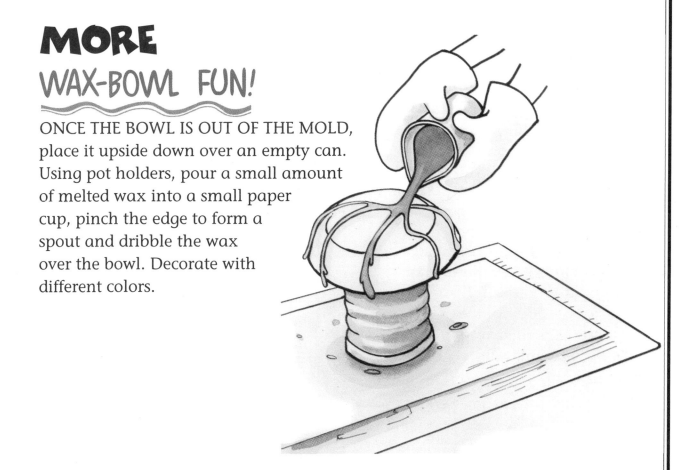

HURRICANE CANDLE

A hurricane candle *is actually an outer wax shell with a smaller candle such as a small votive candle set inside. It gets its name from the way the shell protects the inside candle from strong winds or drafts. The inner candle gives off a softened glow.*

You can place small decorative objects in the wax shell, if you like, and the candlelight will illuminate the outlines. Once you've scooped out the inside wax, however, the shell will dry quickly, so you must have your objects ready and push them into place quickly.

WHAT YOU NEED

Newspaper
Waxed paper
Pan with lid
Melting can
Electric burner
Paraffin wax (please have an
    adult help you melt and pour the wax)
Candy/deep-fry thermometer
Container for mold
Nonstick cooking spray
Spoon
Butter knife
Scissors
Stearine
Color (crayon or candle dye), optional
Fragrance oil, optional
Decorations, such as small erasers,
    shells, beads, marbles, potpourri,
    charms, nuts and bolts (optional)

TRICKS OF THE TRADE
Don't melt the walls!

Choose a container at least 4" to 5" (10 to 12.5 cm) across for the mold. This way, the lit candle inside won't melt your hurricane walls. Milk cartons (1/2 gallon/2 L) and pint-size (500 ml) ice-cream cartons work very well.

WHAT YOU DO

1. **Follow steps 1 through 6** of
the Basic Molded Candle
(pages 21 to 22). You won't
need to set up the wick.
Let cool 20 to 30 minutes.

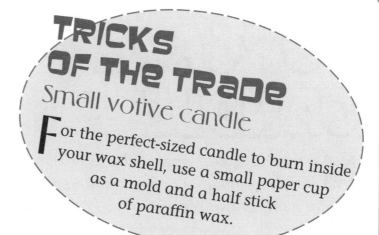

TRICKS OF THE TRADE

Small votive candle

For the perfect-sized candle to burn inside your wax shell, use a small paper cup as a mold and a half stick of paraffin wax.

2. When you see the wax starting to dry around the edges,
carefully scoop out the soft wax in the middle, leaving
walls about ½" (1 cm) thick (page 58, step 2).

3. **For a plain shell:** Smooth the wax walls with the butter
knife or your finger (the wax will be warm but not too
hot to touch and the wax will
peel right off your fingers).

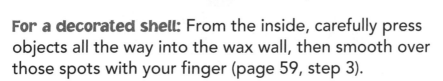

For a decorated shell: From the inside, carefully press
objects all the way into the wax wall, then smooth over
those spots with your finger (page 59, step 3).

Let the shell dry completely.

4. **To remove the mold,** gently pull it away
from the hardened wax.

CUPCAKE CANDLE

Mold a "cupcake" right in the foil baking cup! Easy to whip up a dozen in different colors and they're a real crowd-pleaser — you can see why these are my favorite party favors! Brown wax set in a mini-muffin cup looks just like a peanut-butter cup!

WHAT YOU NEED

Supplies for the Basic Molded Candle (page 20)
Silver foil baking cups, for mold/holder
Skewer
Scraps of beeswax, optional

WHAT YOU DO

1. **Follow steps 1 through 6** of the Basic Molded Candle (pages 21 to 22). If melting different colors, melt each one in a separate can. When you get to step 4, prime the wick if necessary but don't secure it in the mold.

Once the candle hardens, use the skewer to poke a hole through the center of the shape. Pull the wick through and cut it off about 1/2" (1 cm) above the top of the candle.

2. **Decorate the cupcakes:** Spread some whipped wax on the top of the candle. Decorate with scraps of beeswax, or dribble melted wax in a contrasting color over the top.

iNDEX